MOTEL PRAYERS

By Nesi Jordan

Dedication

I dedicate Motel Prayers to my Lord and Savior, Jesus Christ, for providing a space of peace, prayer, and divine encounters through His Word. This story is a testament to His unchanging faithfulness and the transformative power of His love.

To all the readers and listeners, thank you for taking this journey with me. May this book inspire you to seek the Lord in every season of your life and allow His light to shine through you, guiding others toward Him. Remember, it is through His Word and Spirit that we find hope, healing, and purpose.

"Your faithfulness endures to all generations;
You have established the earth, and it stands fast."
— Psalm 119:90

With love and gratitude,
Nesi Jordan

Table of Contents

Dedication iii

Chapter 1: The Sanctuary of Hopes and Blessings 1

Chapter 2: Willie's Awakening 5

Chapter 3: The Music of Redemption 8

Chapter 4: The Shadow of Redemption 11

Chapter 5: The Promise After Prom 14

Chapter 6: A New Current 17

Chapter 7: Light in the Darkness 21

Chapter 8: Be Still and Listen 24

Chapter 9: Truth in the Quiet 27

Chapter 10: Hosanna Moment 30

Chapter 1

The Sanctuary of Hopes and Blessings

"Heavenly Father, we thank You for this sanctuary—a place where Your Spirit moves, bringing healing, hope, and restoration. Let every soul who enters here experience Your presence and leave transformed. May Your will continue to flow through this place, touching lives in miraculous ways. Amen."

The Heaven's Rest Motel wasn't much to look at from the outside. The faded paint, rusted signage, and cracked asphalt parking lot made it appear like any other roadside stop. But to those who stayed within its walls, it was so much more.

It had been dubbed "The Sanctuary of Hopes and Blessings" by those who had experienced its inexplicable peace and miraculous transformations. Stories about the motel had spread far and wide, whispered among travelers, passed along in testimonies at church gatherings, and even written about in obscure blogs and newsletters.

The miracles didn't begin with grand gestures or overt displays of power. Instead, they unfolded quietly, almost imperceptibly, in the hearts and minds of those who entered its rooms.

The Backstory of Heaven's Rest

Years ago, the land on which the motel now stood was barren and overlooked. Locals said it had been cursed—nothing would grow there, and no business could thrive. It was an unassuming patch of dirt off a lonely highway, forgotten by most.

That all changed when an unknown benefactor purchased the land. No one knew much about the owner, not even the staff who managed the property. The owner's presence was felt, not seen. Mysterious, handwritten instructions would arrive in envelopes, directing the staff on renovations, hiring decisions, and even which scriptures to place in each room.

The instructions were always signed the same way: *"For His Glory."*

From the moment the first foundation was laid, there was something different about the place. Construction workers reported feeling an unexplainable peace while they worked. Several of them gave their lives to Christ after random conversations with strangers who just happened to walk by.

By the time the motel opened its doors, it wasn't just a business—it was a ministry.

The Miracles Within

In Room 7, a blind man named Joseph stayed one stormy night, hoping to find refuge from the pouring rain. He had given up on life, feeling abandoned and useless. But in the silence of his room, a vision of light filled his mind, and he heard the words: *"Your faith has healed you."* The next morning, he opened his eyes to a world of color and light he hadn't seen in over a decade.

In Room 3, a woman named Angela checked in, hiding from an abusive relationship. She had spent years feeling unworthy and broken. During the night, she opened the Bible placed on the nightstand and read the story of the woman with the issue of blood. Angela felt a warmth course through her body and a voice whispered, *"You are my daughter, and your faith has made you whole."* She left the motel not only physically stronger but with the courage to reclaim her life.

Room 12 became a turning point for a man named Marcus, who had been paralyzed from the waist down. He had spent years sitting in despair, much like the paralyzed man at the pool of Bethesda. That night, he dreamed of a figure telling him to stand. When he awoke, he hesitated but felt compelled to try. To his astonishment, his legs moved.

A Divine Presence

The staff often spoke of unusual occurrences they couldn't explain. The maid, Jessica, recalled entering a room to find it glowing softly, as though illuminated by an unseen light source. She'd pause at the threshold, feeling an overwhelming sense of peace before quietly closing the door.

The motel's handyman, Gerald, once tried to fix a flickering light in Room 8. When he climbed the ladder and reached out, he heard a voice say, *"My grace is sufficient for you."* Startled, he looked around but saw no one. The light stopped flickering on its own.

Even the local pastor, who had stayed at the motel after his church burned down, reported a divine encounter. Sitting in his room, he had been crying out to God for guidance when he felt a hand on his shoulder. He turned to find no one there, but the peace that washed over him was undeniable.

The Owner Who Was Never There

Despite the countless stories of transformation, no one had ever met the owner. The staff managed the property with meticulous care, following the mysterious instructions that arrived like clockwork.

The guests often asked about the owner, curious about the person behind the motel's supernatural reputation.

"The owner isn't here physically," the clerk would explain with a knowing smile. "But He sees all and makes sure everything is in place."

Over time, guests began to understand: the true Owner wasn't just a person—it was the presence of God Himself, working through this unassuming motel to reach His people.

A Meeting Place for the Spirit

The Heaven's Rest Motel became a modern-day well, much like the one where Jesus met the Samaritan woman. Travelers came burdened, weary, and thirsty for something they couldn't name. And like the woman at the well, they left with their cups overflowing.

For some, it was healing. For others, it was clarity, peace, or the courage to face their struggles. Each encounter was unique, but all carried the unmistakable mark of the Holy Spirit.

The Sanctuary's Promise

As the years passed, the motel remained a beacon of hope. People came from far and wide, not because of its appearance or amenities, but because of the stories they'd heard. They came seeking what they couldn't find elsewhere: the touch of the Divine.

In a world full of chaos, Heaven's Rest Motel stood as a reminder that God's presence could transform the ordinary into the extraordinary.

"Lord, thank You for using this place as a sanctuary of hope and blessings. May all who enter here encounter Your love, healing, and grace. Let Your Spirit continue to flow, touching lives and drawing them closer to You. Amen."

Chapter 2

Willie's Awakening

The narrator's voice floated gently through the stillness of the motel, like the lingering scent of something divine. It was not the owner of the motel, for no one had ever seen or spoken to them. Yet, an undeniable presence filled the air, carried by words whispered in prayer.

"Father, You know every traveler who walks through these doors. Some arrive by accident, others by design, and still others out of sheer desperation. But You meet each one where they are. Tonight, Lord, a man named Willie has come He is weary in body and soul, even if he does not know it yet. Use this room, these walls, and the words within to show him the truth he has been running from. Amen."

Willie Maize yawned as he gripped the steering wheel of his sleek black sedan. The car, like his custom-tailored suit, was a symbol of his success. A Wall Street stockbroker, Willie had spent the better part of his life turning risks into rewards, believing that money was the only power that truly mattered. But now, his exhaustion was catching up with him.

The GPS had directed him to a desolate stretch of road where a single, unassuming motel stood. Its faded sign read, "Heaven's Rest," glowing faintly under the flicker of an old neon bulb. Willie had pulled into the parking lot, intending to close his eyes for a brief moment in the comfort of his car.

The sharp tap on his driver's side window jolted him awake. A burly security guard stood there, his flashlight cutting through the darkness. Willie rolled the window down an inch, just enough to hear.

"You can't park here without a room," the guard said firmly.

"I'm just resting my eyes," Willie replied with a wave of his hand, his tone dismissive.

The guard crossed his arms. "Policy's policy. You either rent a room or leave the premises."

Willie groaned inwardly. Arguing wasn't worth the effort, not when all he wanted was an hour of uninterrupted rest. With reluctance, he climbed out of the car and made his way to the front desk, muttering under his breath about ridiculous rules.

The room was small but oddly inviting, with warm lighting and a faint scent of lavender. Willie tossed his suitcase onto the bed, removed his shoes, and loosened his tie. It wasn't until he stepped into the shower, letting the water wash over him, that he noticed something unusual: the wallpaper.

Bible verses. Everywhere.

From *Psalm 23* to *John 3:16*, the words surrounded him like a chorus of silent witnesses. Willie felt a twinge of discomfort but shrugged it off. *Just a quirky decorating choice,* he thought.

When he emerged from the bathroom, his curiosity got the better of him. He examined the room more closely. The TV offered only two channels, both playing gospel programs. A Bible sat on the nightstand, its cover well-worn. Next to it was a journal pad and a pen.

Willie hesitated, then picked up the Bible. It opened to a bookmarked page: the story of King Saul. He skimmed the verses, his interest piqued by the tale of a man who had everything but lost it all due to his pride and disobedience.

Pride... The word hit Willie like a punch to the gut.

He sat down on the edge of the bed, the journal pad now in his hands. The first page had a simple question written at the top: *"What would you say to God if He were listening?"*

For the first time in years, Willie allowed himself to be honest—not with his clients, not with his colleagues, but with himself. His pen hovered over the blank page before he began to write.

"God, I've spent my whole life chasing what I thought mattered: money, power, respect. I thought those things made me untouchable, but tonight, I feel small. I don't

know why I'm here, but if You can hear me... I want to change. I'm tired of running. Forgive me for my arrogance, my pride. Help me start over."

Willie didn't know how long he sat there, but when he finally put the pen down, a strange peace filled the room. It wasn't the kind of peace that came from a successful deal or a hefty paycheck. This was different—pure, unshakable.

He knelt by the bed, his head bowed. "Jesus, I don't know much about You, but if You can take someone like Saul and give him a second chance, maybe You can do the same for me. I surrender."

As Willie drifted off to sleep, the room seemed to glow softly, though he didn't notice. And as the motel fell silent once more, the narrator whispered a prayer of thanksgiving.

"One down, Lord. Many more to go.
Amen."

Chapter 3

The Music of Redemption

Elijah Franklin tightened his grip on the battered violin case as he stepped into the lobby of the Heaven's Rest Motel. His fingers trembled—not from the cold, but from the weight of his exhaustion.

"One room," he rasped, his voice barely audible over the hum of the old ceiling fan.

The clerk handed him a key with a knowing smile. "Room 9. You'll find what you're looking for."

Elijah didn't respond. He trudged down the narrow hall, his boots scuffing the floor with every step. The glow of the neon sign outside seeped through the thin curtains of his room, casting a faint pink light on the walls.

Inside, the same peculiar decor greeted him. Bible verses adorned the wallpaper, and an aged Bible rested on the nightstand. He sighed, setting the violin case down gently.

"Another one of these holy motels," he muttered, shrugging off his coat.

Elijah's career as a violinist had once shown promise. He had been a prodigy, performing in symphonies across the country before he turned twenty-five. But now, at thirty-nine, the sheen of his early success had dulled. A life of touring, bad decisions, and broken relationships had taken its toll.

He opened the violin case and stared at the instrument inside. The varnish was worn, the strings frayed. Just like me, he thought bitterly.

After a quick shower, Elijah sat on the edge of the bed, staring at the wallpaper. One verse caught his eye:

"Make a joyful noise unto the Lord, all the earth: make a loud noise,
and rejoice, and sing praise." – Psalm 98:4

He laughed bitterly. "Yeah, sure. What noise can I make that anyone wants to hear?"

He reached for the Bible on the nightstand but stopped short when he noticed the journal beside it. Curious, he opened it and saw an entry written in neat cursive:

"The Lord is near to the brokenhearted and saves the crushed in
spirit." – Psalm 34:18

Elijah felt something stir within him. He flipped through more entries, each one a testimony of someone who had stayed in this room and encountered God. As the night wore on, Elijah picked up his violin. He hadn't played in months, but now, the bow felt right in his hand. He began to play softly, his fingers finding a hymn his mother used to sing:

"Great is Thy faithfulness, O God my Father…"

The melody filled the room, mingling with the words on the wallpaper and the testimonies in the journal.

The next morning, Elijah turned on the TV and saw a gospel broadcast. A pastor spoke directly into the camera.

"God gives each of us a gift, but sometimes we lose sight of the Giver. If you're feeling lost, remember this: He's waiting for you to return. He never stops calling your name."

The pastor's words echoed in Elijah's heart. He set the violin down and knelt beside the bed.

"God," he whispered, his voice cracking. "I don't know if You're still there. But if You are… I'm tired of running. Please… take what's left of me and make something new."

When Elijah left the motel later that day, the violin case felt lighter in his hand. He didn't have all the answers, but he had something he hadn't felt in years: hope.

"Thank You, Lord, for giving this weary musician a reason to play again. Another story, another soul. Amen."

Chapter 4

The Shadow of Redemption

"Heavenly Father, we thank You for Your relentless love and patience with us when we run from Your calling. Let this chapter remind us of Your presence that is never absent, even when we feel unworthy. Lord, may Your truth reveal that You are always seen through Your work, even when hidden from view. Amen."

The Heaven's Rest Motel stood quiet under the silver glow of the moon. Pastor Charles Payne sat on the edge of the bed in Room 12, staring at the unopened bottle of whiskey on the nightstand.

Five years sober, and here I am, he thought bitterly. The worn Bible beside the bottle felt like a silent rebuke. He'd brought it out of habit, but lately, its pages seemed closed to him.

Charles had pastored a small congregation for almost a decade, pouring his heart into every sermon, every prayer, and every hospital visit. Yet all of that crumbled when someone from his church unearthed his past—a history of mistakes and brokenness that he thought he'd buried at the altar years ago.

He ran.

He left behind his flock, his ministry, and the memory of his grandfather, Pastor Kelvin Payne, a towering figure of faith who had been Charles's hero. His grandfather had built their family's legacy in the church, a legacy that now felt like a heavy chain around Charles's neck.

Unable to sleep, Charles decided to grab ice from the machine outside. The night air was cool, and the sound of cicadas filled the silence. He carried the ice bucket, his steps slow and deliberate, as if dragging the weight of his shame.

As he reached the ice machine, his hand trembled, the bucket clinking against the machine. He stared at the ice tumbling out, thinking of how cold and distant his heart felt.

Then a shadow passed across the ground, and Charles froze. The ice bucket slipped from his hand, hitting the pavement with a dull thud. The spilled water began to spread across the ground, shimmering under the faint glow of the motel lights.

And then, the impossible.

The spilled water pooled into a shape—first vague, then clearer—until a man appeared. The figure was radiant, not of flesh but light, and yet it seemed solid enough to feel the weight of Charles's gaze.

The pastor staggered back, his heart pounding. "What… what is this?" he whispered.

The figure didn't speak but pointed toward the Bible verses etched into the motel's wallpaper, visible even from where Charles stood outside.

"But the Lord sent out a great wind into the sea, and there was a mighty tempest in the sea, so that the ship was like to be broken."
— Jonah 1:4

Charles stumbled back into his room, his hands shaking as he opened the Bible to the story of Jonah. He read through tear-blurred eyes, his heart pounding with every word. Jonah, too, had run. He had tried to escape God's calling, only to be swallowed by a great fish and carried to the very place he had resisted going.

The figure remained in the room, silent but present, as Charles read.

"I've been running," Charles whispered. "I ran from my flock, my calling… even You."

The figure nodded.

"I thought I couldn't face them. They found out about my past, and I… I couldn't stand the shame. My grandfather… he'd be so disappointed."

For the first time, the figure spoke, its voice like a gentle wind. "Your worth was never in your past, but in your surrender to Me. Your grandfather knew that. Now you must, too."

Charles fell to his knees, tears streaming down his face. "Lord, I'm sorry. I'm so sorry for running. I'm tired of running. Please… forgive me."

The next morning, Charles woke with a renewed sense of purpose. The bottle of whiskey sat untouched on the nightstand. He packed his things and grabbed his Bible, the pages now open to Jonah's story.

As he left the motel, the words of the narrator's prayer echoed in his heart:

"Though the owner is never seen, his presence is always felt. Amen."

Charles knew he had to return—not just to his congregation, but to his faith.

He drove back toward his small church, the words of Jonah's story still fresh in his mind. Sometimes, God sends storms not to punish us but to redirect us.

*"Thank You, Lord, for reminding this weary shepherd that Your love
never lets us go. Another story, another soul. Amen."*

Chapter 5

The Promise After Prom

"Heavenly Father, we come to You with grateful hearts, asking for Your guidance in honoring You with our lives and decisions. Let this chapter remind us that purity is a gift we give not just to ourselves but to You. May Your presence in the unseen be felt as we walk in Your light. Amen."

The night after prom was supposed to be magical, or at least that's what Robyn and Jessie had thought. Both 18, high school seniors, and full of dreams, they had rented Room 17 at the Heaven's Rest Motel. It was a simple plan: share a night together before the uncertainties of college and the future.

But from the moment they walked into the room, something felt different.

The motel room was quiet, save for the faint hum of the air conditioner. Robyn sat nervously on the edge of the bed, smoothing the fabric of her prom dress, while Jessie fiddled with the TV remote.

Every channel seemed to play the same thing: gospel messages, worship songs, or movies about faith. Jessie groaned and turned the TV off, tossing the remote onto the bed.

"That's... weird," he said, scratching his head.

Robyn laughed nervously. "Maybe it's a sign," she said half-jokingly.

They both knew why they were there. The night was supposed to be about taking the next step in their relationship, but now that they were alone, the weight of the moment felt heavier than they'd anticipated.

Jessie walked over to the nightstand and picked up the well-worn Bible. He flipped it open, his eyes landing on a verse about Mary:

"And the angel said unto her, Fear not, Mary: for thou hast found favour with God. And, behold, thou shalt conceive in thy womb, and bring forth a son, and shalt call his name Jesus."
– Luke 1:30-31

He paused, then read it aloud. "Hey, Robyn, listen to this…"

For the next hour, they sat together, the Bible open between them, as they read the story of the Virgin Mary.

"She was so young," Robyn said, her voice soft. "She trusted God completely, even though what He asked of her was… well, huge."

Jessie nodded. "And she honored Him with her body, her whole life. That's incredible."

A quiet moment passed between them. Jessie reached for Robyn's hand, his voice gentle. "Do you think… we should wait?"

Robyn looked at him, her eyes glistening. "I was just thinking the same thing. I mean, if we really love each other, and if we want to do this right… maybe we should save this for after we're married."

Jessie smiled. "Then let's do it. Let's make a promise—to each other and to God—that we'll wait. And when we graduate, we'll come back here as husband and wife."

That night, instead of crossing a line they weren't ready for, they prayed together for the first time. They asked God to bless their relationship and to guide them as they finished high school and planned their future.

The wallpaper scriptures seemed to glow in the soft light of the room. One verse in particular stood out to them:

"For I know the plans I have for you, declares the Lord, plans for welfare and not for evil, to give you a future and a hope."
– Jeremiah 29:11

Robyn traced the words with her finger. "This feels right," she said.

"It does," Jessie agreed.

A year later, true to their word, Robyn and Jessie returned to the Heaven's Rest Motel, this time as newlyweds. Room 17 felt almost sacred to them now, a place where they had made a promise and kept it.

As they unpacked, Robyn noticed something on the nightstand—a tiny baby shoe, left there as if by accident. She picked it up, her heart racing.

Jessie smiled. "Maybe it's another sign," he said.

Robyn laughed, tears in her eyes. "You think?"

The following month, Robyn found out she was pregnant. The seed of their love—and their faith—had blossomed into a new life.

"Thank You, Lord, for the strength to honor You and each other.
Another story, another soul. Amen."

Chapter 6

A New Current

"Heavenly Father, we pray for clarity and courage to stand firm in Your truth, even when it's difficult. Let Your Holy Spirit guide us beyond fear and doubt, helping us walk the path You have set before us. May this chapter inspire hearts to trust You without borders. Amen."

Travis Smithway pulled into the parking lot of the Heaven's Rest Motel just before midnight. The drive had been long and silent, with nothing but the rhythm of the tires on the highway to keep him company.

As a college senior and a competitive swimmer, Travis had always been known for his discipline and focus. But lately, he felt adrift, unsure of who he was outside the water.

He checked into Room 8, tossing his duffel bag onto the bed. The wallpaper caught his attention immediately—Bible verses printed in a simple, elegant script. He noticed one that seemed to leap off the wall:

"Trust in the Lord with all your heart, and lean not on your own understanding." – Proverbs 3:5

Travis sighed and sat down on the edge of the bed, scrolling through his phone.

A notification popped up—a comment on an article featuring his potential rise as a professional swimmer. The comment was from a former friend, someone from the tight-knit group he had distanced himself from because their values didn't align with his own.

The words stung: "Travis thinks he's too good for us now. Wonder what his new 'holy' friends would think if they really knew him."

Travis felt a wave of frustration and hurt. He had parted ways with those friends because their choices and beliefs conflicted with his own growing convictions. Yet, their opinions still had a grip on him.

He turned off his phone and glanced at the nightstand. There lay an open Bible, and beside it, a journal. Something about it drew him in. He picked up the Bible, letting its pages fall open. His eyes landed on the story of Sodom and Gomorrah in Genesis 19.

He read about Lot, a righteous man living in a place consumed by sin. God's angels warned him to flee the city before it was destroyed. But what struck Travis most was Lot's wife—how she looked back, unable to let go of the life she had left behind, and was turned into a pillar of salt.

The weight of the story hit him.

Travis whispered, "Am I looking back, too? Holding onto what I know isn't right because I'm afraid of what they'll think of me?"

He placed the Bible down and lay back on the bed, staring at the ceiling. His mind replayed memories of his old group of friends—jokes they made, parties they invited him to, and the pressure they put on him to conform to their lifestyle.

He had tried to keep the peace, to go along without fully participating, but it became clear he couldn't. Travis felt like he was drowning, pulled in by their choices while trying to hold on to his faith.

A faint knock at the door startled him. Opening it, he found no one, only a small envelope placed neatly on the ground. He picked it up and opened it inside.

The note read:

"Do not conform to the pattern of this world but be transformed by the renewing of your mind. Then you will be able to test and approve what God's will is—His good, pleasing, and perfect will."
– Romans 12:2

The words pierced his heart. He felt the tears come before he could stop them. Travis whispered, "God, are You trying to tell me something? I need to know what to do. I'm scared to lose people I care about, but I'm more scared to lose You."

As he wrestled with the thought, a familiar song played faintly from the TV: *"Spirit lead me where my trust is without borders..."*

It was *Oceans* by Hillsong United. The lyrics stirred something deep within him. He thought of Peter stepping out of the boat to walk on water toward Jesus, trusting completely despite the storm raging around him.

The imagery felt personal, like God was calling him to step out of his own boat, leaving behind comfort, fear, and the opinions of others.

Travis closed his eyes, his voice barely a whisper. "God, I don't know what You're calling me to do. I just know I can't stay in this place of fear and compromise. Show me the way forward."

A warmth flooded his heart—a sense of peace he hadn't felt in months. He opened his eyes and reached for the journal. Inside was a single handwritten note:

"Walk in faith, not fear. The currents of life will try to pull you away, but keep your eyes on Jesus. He will never let you sink."

The next morning, Travis stood by the motel's small pool, staring at the still water. He thought about the decisions ahead—whether to pursue a professional swimming career, how to stand firm in his faith, and what it meant to truly trust God.

A verse from the wallpaper lingered in his mind:

"But seek first the kingdom of God and His righteousness, and all these things shall be added to you."
– Matthew 6:33

As he walked away from the pool, Travis felt lighter, as if the weight of expectation had been lifted.

He whispered a promise to God: "I'll follow You, no matter what. Even if I'm alone."

For the first time in a long while, Travis felt free—not just to swim, but to live.

"Thank You, Lord, for calling us out of the boat and into the waters of faith. Help us to trust You beyond borders and walk boldly in Your truth. Another story, another soul. Amen."

Chapter 7

Light in the Darkness

"Heavenly Father, we lift up this traveler to You. Whatever darkness they are battling, let Your light break through and guide them to freedom. May this chapter serve as a beacon for those wrestling with unseen forces, reminding them that no battle is too great for You. Amen."

Billy Watkins arrived at the Heaven's Rest Motel with heavy eyes and an even heavier heart. His black hoodie hung over his face like a curtain, shielding him from the world—or perhaps the world from him. He had driven for hours without a destination, fleeing an invisible torment that had plagued him for years.

The desk clerk handed him a key with a smile, but Billy barely noticed. He trudged down the dimly lit hall to Room 9, a backpack slung over one shoulder. Once inside, he locked the door, dropped his bag on the floor, and sat on the edge of the bed.

Billy's hands trembled as he reached into his bag and pulled out a small radio. It was battered, its silver edges worn from years of use. To anyone else, it looked like an outdated relic. But to Billy, it was more than that—it was a lifeline.

The radio crackled to life as he turned the dial. Static hissed before settling on a faint, soothing voice reading scripture:

"For God has not given us a spirit of fear, but of power and of love and of a sound mind." – 2 Timothy 1:7

Billy closed his eyes and let the words wash over him. For as long as he could remember, there had been voices in his mind—dark, accusing, and relentless. They whispered lies, fed his fears, and drove him to the brink of despair. But the radio, with its calming scriptures and hymns, was his anchor.

All through the night, Billy spoke aloud, as if responding to someone unseen. His words alternated between fervent prayers and bursts of anger.

"Why won't you leave me alone?" he shouted at one point, pacing the room. Then, softer: "God, are You even there? I can't keep living like this."

As the hours passed, something began to shift. The radio continued to play, and Billy felt an unfamiliar warmth settle over him. It was as though the words weren't just coming from the speakers but were being spoken directly to his heart.

The next morning, Jessica, one of the motel's maids, noticed the *Do Not Disturb* sign hanging on Billy's door. She hesitated, then moved on to the next room. But something about Room 9 lingered in her mind.

Later, while taking a break, Jessica passed by the door again. This time, she felt a strange pull, as though she were being drawn to it.

The door seemed to glow faintly, a soft, golden light that pulsed like a heartbeat. Jessica froze, her breath catching in her throat.

"What is this?" she whispered, clutching her cleaning cart for support.

Jessica wasn't particularly religious, but she had grown up in church. Her grandmother used to tell her stories from the Bible, and one of them came rushing back to her now: the story of Moses encountering the burning bush, where God's presence made the ordinary extraordinary.

Her curiosity piqued, Jessica leaned closer to the door. She could hear faint murmurs from within, Billy's voice alternating between pleading and proclaiming scripture.

That night, Jessica couldn't shake what she had seen and heard. As she sat in the breakroom, she dialed her husband, Sam.

"Hey," she said, her voice trembling.

"Jessica? What's wrong?"

"Sam... I think I saw something today. At work. A sign or... I don't know."

"What kind of sign?"

Jessica hesitated, then explained everything—the glowing door, the scriptures, the man inside who seemed to be battling something unseen.

Sam was silent for a moment. Then he said, "You know I've been struggling with... with my own demons. Maybe this is God's way of showing you how to help me."

Meanwhile, in Room 9, Billy sat cross-legged on the floor, the radio still playing softly. He felt a strange peace, though he couldn't explain why.

The story of the demon-possessed boy in the Bible had played earlier, and Billy had clung to every word. Jesus had cast out the spirit, not because of the father's perfection but because of his faith, however small it was.

Billy whispered, "God, if You could do that for him, could You do it for me too?"

The glow around Billy's door began to intensify, visible even to passersby outside the motel. Some stopped and stared, while others hurried away, unsettled by what they couldn't understand.

Jessica returned to the door, this time with Sam. He stood in awe of the light, his skepticism melting into something else—hope.

"I think we're supposed to pray," Jessica said, reaching for his hand.

Together, they prayed aloud, asking God to deliver Billy from whatever was tormenting him and to bring healing and freedom.

Inside the room, Billy felt a sudden rush of emotion, like a dam breaking inside him. He fell to his knees, tears streaming down his face as he cried out, "Jesus, help me! I can't do this alone!"

The radio crackled, and a voice said clearly, *"Come to Me, all you who are weary and burdened, and I will give you rest."* – Matthew 11:28

Billy felt something leave him—a heaviness he hadn't even realized he was carrying. In its place was a lightness, a peace that was almost tangible.

As the glow around the door faded, Jessica and Sam knew their prayers had been answered. They knocked gently, and Billy opened the door, his face tear-streaked but radiant.

"Who are you?" he asked, his voice trembling.

"Just people who wanted to help," Jessica said, smiling.

Billy nodded, understanding that God had orchestrated this moment.

That night, three people left the motel changed: Billy, free from his torment; Jessica, with renewed faith; and Sam, ready to confront his own struggles with the hope that healing was possible.

"Thank You, Lord, for being the light in our darkness. Thank You for delivering us from what binds us and for using ordinary people to show Your extraordinary love. Another story, another soul. Amen."

Chapter 8

Be Still and Listen

"Heavenly Father, we lift up Raina Brookes, a woman who carries the weight of her world on her shoulders. Teach her to find rest in You and to hear Your still, small voice amidst the noise of life. May she discover the peace that only comes from sitting at Your feet. Amen."

Raina Brookes pulled her car into the gravel lot of the Heaven's Rest Motel, exhaustion etched into her face. She stared at the flickering neon sign through her windshield, debating whether she should just drive home.

Home was 45 minutes away, but she only had three hours before her alarm would buzz her back to life. With a deep sigh, she grabbed her bag and headed inside.

The desk clerk gave her a key to Room 11, and Raina trudged down the hallway, her shoes scuffing against the worn carpet. The motel was quiet, save for the hum of a vending machine and the faint murmur of a TV in another room.

Once inside, Raina tossed her bag onto the chair and fell onto the bed, not bothering to change out of her work uniform. The weight of the day pressed down on her like a heavy blanket. Between her double shifts at the diner, her online classes, and juggling family obligations, Raina hadn't had a moment to breathe in months.

She stared at the ceiling, her mind racing with tomorrow's to-do list.

"Bills to pay, essays to write, Mom's doctor appointment, groceries for the week…" she muttered, her voice trailing off.

A gust of wind rattled the window, and the room suddenly plunged into darkness.

"Are you kidding me?" Raina groaned, fumbling for her phone. She turned on the flashlight, its beam bouncing off the walls. The motel's power must have gone out, leaving her room eerily quiet.

Raina grabbed her bag to dig for a charger, but her fingers brushed against something unexpected—a Bible. She pulled it out, its edges worn from use. It must have been left by the motel.

She stared at it for a moment, then tossed it onto the nightstand with a scoff. "No time for that," she muttered.

Raina's phone buzzed with a low battery warning. She groaned again, realizing she hadn't packed her charger. Defeated, she slumped back onto the bed.

The room was dark and silent, forcing her to confront a stillness she wasn't used to. It reminded her of the story her grandmother used to tell about Martha and Mary from the Bible.

Martha had been so consumed with preparing everything for Jesus that she missed the point of His visit. Meanwhile, Mary had simply sat at His feet, listening to His words.

Raina could still hear her grandmother's voice: *"Don't be so busy doing that you forget being, Raina. Sometimes, the best thing you can do is sit still and listen."*

With nothing else to do, Raina reached for the Bible. She opened it randomly, her fingers landing on Luke 10:41-42:

> *"Martha, Martha," the Lord answered, "you are worried and upset*
> *about many things, but few things are needed—or indeed only one.*
> *Mary has chosen what is better, and it will not be taken*
> *away from her."*

The words hit Raina like a jolt. She closed the Bible and leaned back, staring at the ceiling again.

"Am I like Martha?" she whispered. "Too busy to even notice what really matters?"

A memory surfaced: her grandmother praying over her as a child, asking God to guide her path. Raina had grown up in church, but as life got busier, her faith had taken a backseat. Now, sitting alone in the quiet, she felt a pang of longing for the peace she used to know.

She glanced at the clock. It was 3:30 a.m. With a sigh, she closed her eyes and whispered, "God, I don't even know what to say. I'm just...tired. I can't keep doing this."

For the first time in years, Raina sat in silence. No distractions, no to-do lists—just the sound of her breathing and the faint rustle of the wind outside.

A strange warmth enveloped her, like a gentle embrace. It wasn't loud or overwhelming, but it was unmistakable.

"Be still," a voice seemed to whisper in her heart. "And know that I am God."

Tears welled up in Raina's eyes. She hadn't realized how much she needed this moment—this pause, this reminder that she didn't have to carry everything on her own.

When the power flickered back on, Raina didn't move. The clock on the nightstand glowed softly, and the hum of the air conditioning returned. But Raina stayed still, letting the peace wash over her.

She made a decision right then: life couldn't keep going the way it was. She would carve out time to rest, to listen, to reconnect with the God she had pushed aside for so long.

The next morning, Raina arrived at the diner with a renewed sense of purpose. Her coworkers noticed the change immediately.

"You look...different," one of them said.

Raina smiled. "Just trying to keep the main thing the main thing," she replied. She didn't explain further, but she didn't need to.

"Lord, thank You for meeting us in the stillness. Help us to slow down, to sit at Your feet, and to remember what truly matters. May we, like Mary, choose what is better and find peace in Your presence. Amen."

Chapter 9

Truth in the Quiet

"Father, You see it all—the heavy burdens, the unspoken truths, and the wounds only You can heal. Tonight, Rose and Pam have come to this place, carrying years of love tangled with secrets. Lord, let Your Word shine like a lamp in the darkness, guiding them both toward the truth that sets free. May their hearts be softened, their spirits renewed, and their lives transformed. Amen."

Rose Adams opened the door to Room 7, balancing a duffel bag in one hand while supporting her elderly mother, Pam, with the other. Pam moved slowly, her frail frame leaning heavily on a wooden cane.

"Let me get the chair, Mom," Rose said, setting the bag down to guide Pam into the room's armchair.

Pam smiled faintly, her weathered face showing more exhaustion than gratitude. "I'm fine, sweetheart. You've done enough today."

Rose tried to return the smile, but the weight of her responsibilities dimmed its light. At 27, she was a young woman with an old soul. Caring for Pam had become her full-time job—one that left little room for anything else. She couldn't hold a steady job, let alone plan her own life. But she loved Pam. That love kept her going, even on days when her patience wore thin.

The room was quiet except for the hum of the air conditioner. As Rose unpacked their essentials, she noticed the wallpaper. *Bible verses again?* she thought, recalling the last time they'd stayed at a Heaven's Rest Motel. She didn't mind—it was oddly comforting.

"Mom, why don't you rest a bit? I'll grab us some dinner," Rose suggested.

Pam nodded, but her gaze lingered on the wallpaper, her lips moving as if silently reading the scriptures.

While Rose stepped out to the nearby diner, her phone buzzed. The name on the screen stopped her in her tracks: **Dad.**

Her heart raced. Her "dad"—the man she'd believed was long lost to her—had found her through an ancestry site she'd joined on a whim years ago.

"Hello?" she answered hesitantly.

"Rose?" The voice was deep, warm, and unmistakably nervous.

"Yes… this is Rose."

"This is… well, I'm your father, Daniel Adams. I've been looking for you for a long time. I… I found you through the DNA match on Ancestry."

Rose froze. The words didn't seem real. She'd grown up without a father, raised solely by Pam, who had never spoken much about her past.

"I… I'm at a loss," Rose said, her voice trembling.

Daniel hesitated. "If it's not too much, I'd love to meet you. I know this is sudden, but I wanted to call and let you know that I've found you."

Rose didn't know what to say. A part of her wanted to hang up, but another part—a deeper, yearning part—needed answers.

"I'll… think about it," she managed before ending the call.

Back in the room, Pam had finished a shower and was now seated on the bed, flipping through the Bible she'd found on the nightstand. The story of Saul's conversion to Paul had caught her attention, and as she read, something stirred deep within her.

Pam looked up as Rose returned. She could see the tension in her daughter's face.

"Everything okay?" Pam asked.

Rose hesitated, then sat down across from her mother. "I got a call… from someone claiming to be my dad. He found me through Ancestry."

Pam's expression froze, and for a moment, the room felt like it had stopped breathing.

"I need to tell you something," Pam said, her voice trembling. "I've been holding this in for years, and I know I owe you the truth."

Rose's stomach churned. "What are you talking about?"

Pam took a deep breath. "You're not… my daughter."

The words hit Rose like a freight train.

"What?"

"You're my nephew's daughter," Pam confessed, tears streaming down her face. "Your parents—your real parents—wanted to raise you, but I… I wouldn't let them. I was the matriarch of the family, always in control. I didn't trust men, and I didn't trust your father, so I took you in. I thought I was doing what was best, but it wasn't. It was selfish."

Rose's mind raced as the pieces of her life began to rearrange themselves.

"All this time…" she whispered, her voice breaking. "All this time, I could have known my parents? My real parents?"

Pam nodded, unable to speak.

The room was silent except for the soft murmur of the TV. A program was playing—a sermon about Saul's transformation into Paul.

The preacher's voice cut through the tension. "Paul was a man who lived in darkness, consumed by pride and hatred. But when he encountered the truth of Christ, his life changed forever. What lies are you holding onto? What truths are you afraid to face?"

Pam wept openly now. "I've been so wrong, Rose. So, so wrong. But tonight, I read about Saul, and I realized if God could forgive him, maybe He could forgive me too. Can you forgive me?"

Rose looked at her mother—no, her aunt—and saw not just the woman who had raised her, but a flawed human being seeking redemption.

"I need time," Rose said softly. "But… I think I can try."

As the night wore on, mother and daughter—bound by love and now freed by truth—sat together, listening to the story of Saul and Paul. Somewhere in that tiny motel room, forgiveness began to take root.

*"Thank You, Lord, for breaking through the lies and bringing
healing where it was needed most. One more soul, one more story.
Amen."*

Chapter 10

Hosanna Moment

"Heavenly Father, let this final chapter of encounters at Heaven's Rest Motel glorify Your name. May it open the eyes of the blind, soften hardened hearts, and reveal the power of Your presence. Let Your Spirit flow through this moment of truth, bringing light into the darkness. Amen."

The Arrival of Oliver Horton

Oliver Horton was not your average news anchor. Known for his unyielding determination to capture the perfect story, he had made a career of exposing the truth—whether people wanted to hear it or not. But lately, his motivations had taken a turn. It wasn't just about the story anymore; it was about climbing the career ladder. Fame, fortune, and recognition consumed his thoughts.

When whispers of the Heaven's Rest Motel reached Oliver, he dismissed them as local folklore. But when the stories wouldn't stop—accounts of miracles, transformations, and divine encounters—his curiosity was piqued. More importantly, he saw an opportunity.

"If I can catch even one miracle on tape," he mused, "I'll be the most talked-about journalist in the country."

A Guarded Secret

Oliver arrived at the motel late in the evening, camera equipment in tow. He checked in under an alias to avoid drawing attention. As he scoped out the property, he noticed a peculiar figure standing near the front desk—a security guard.

The man was tall, with a presence that seemed both commanding and serene. His uniform bore no insignias, and his eyes radiated something Oliver couldn't quite place.

"Hey, have you worked here long?" Oliver asked casually, aiming to strike up a conversation.

The guard looked at him and smiled. "I've been here longer than you'd imagine," he said. His voice was calm but carried an unexplainable weight.

Oliver was about to ask more, but a strange sensation stopped him. The guard's words, though clear, seemed to echo differently in his ears. It wasn't until later that Oliver realized others nearby hadn't understood a single word.

The Tower of Babel Moment

The next morning, Oliver began interviewing guests. To his frustration, no one seemed to have a clear explanation of the events at the motel. "It just happens," one said. "You'll know when it's your turn."

Determined, Oliver set up cameras in the lobby, the parking lot, and even in one of the rooms. He stayed up all night, reviewing footage. But every time he thought he'd captured something extraordinary, the tapes showed only mundane activity.

The guard appeared again, standing in the lobby. Oliver approached him, eager for answers.

"I know something is happening here," Oliver said. "But I can't prove it. Can you help me understand?"

The guard nodded but spoke in a language that sounded foreign—almost otherworldly. Yet Oliver understood every word.

"This place isn't about proof," the guard said. "It's about faith. You seek for the wrong reasons."

Around them, others glanced curiously at the guard, hearing only unintelligible sounds. They shook their heads and walked away, leaving Oliver more perplexed than ever.

A Divine Encounter

That night, Oliver had a dream. In it, he saw himself standing at the gates of a grand city, holding a microphone and camera. He was eager to enter and tell the world about what he saw. But each time he tried, the gates remained closed.

A voice echoed: *"Why do you seek the gates? Is it to glorify Me or yourself?"*

Oliver woke up in a cold sweat. The question lingered in his mind. He realized that his motives had been selfish. He wasn't seeking the truth to honor God—he was seeking it to elevate his own name.

The Heart of the Matter

The next day, Oliver approached the guard again. This time, he came without his camera or microphone.

"I don't understand what's happening here," Oliver admitted. "But I think it's because I've been looking at it all wrong. What does God want me to see?"

The guard's eyes softened. "He wants your heart, Oliver. Not your ambition. Not your accolades. Just your heart."

At that moment, the guard's form seemed to shift, glowing with a light that filled the room. Oliver fell to his knees, overwhelmed by the presence of the Holy Spirit.

Tears streamed down his face as he whispered, "I'm sorry, Lord. Forgive me for my pride and selfishness. I give it all to You. Use me for Your glory."

A New Purpose

From that day forward, Oliver Horton's life changed. No longer did he chase stories for fame or recognition. Instead, he sought to tell stories that glorified God and brought hope to others.

His first assignment after leaving the motel was to cover a community rebuilding project in a storm-ravaged town. This time, before beginning his work, Oliver bowed his head and prayed:

"Lord, guide me in this story. Let it be for Your glory and not mine. Use me as Your instrument."

As Oliver's reputation grew, it wasn't for his charisma or tenacity—it was for his humility and dedication to truth.

The Legacy of Heaven's Rest

The Heaven's Rest Motel continued to be a sanctuary for weary souls. Though the mysterious security guard was never seen again, his presence lingered in the memories of those who had encountered him.

Oliver often returned, not as a journalist, but as a seeker of peace and renewal. Each time, he left with a deeper understanding of God's grace and a heart full of gratitude.

The motel's story became a testament to the transformative power of faith. For every guest who passed through its doors, it served as a reminder that God's glory could be found even in the most unassuming places.

"Hosanna is the highest! Lord, we thank You for the lessons learned and the lives changed through this sanctuary. May all who hear of this place know that it is not the building but Your Spirit that brings hope and healing. To You be all the glory and honor, forever and ever. Amen."